KENSINGTON OVAL

HIGH RD.

WHITEPARK ROAD

BAOBAB ROAD

ROEBUCK STREET

PUBLIC LIBRARY

LAW COURTS

CENTRAL POLICE STATION

OLD SYNAGOGUE

HARRISON COLLEGE

QUEEN'S PARK

ST. MARY'S CHURCH

CHEAPSIDE MARKET

CONSTITUTION ROAD

ST. MICHAEL'S CATHEDRAL

QUEEN'S COLLEGE

CAN VILLAGE

PRINCESS ALICE HWY.

LOWER GREEN BUS STAND

BROAD STREET SHOPPING AREA

PUBLIC BLDGS

TRAFALGAR SQUARE

CONSTITUTION RIVER ROAD

RIVER

MARKET

CAREENAGE

CHAMBERLAIN BRIDGE

SWING BRIDGE

FAIRCHILD ST. BUS STAND

QUEEN ELIZABETH HOSPITAL

N.

Caribbean Sea

BAY STREET

Bridgetown

ST. PATRICKS R.C. CATHEDRAL

For Thomas H. King, Jr.,
an old and good friend without
whose generosity this book
would never have been

Snack in hand, hat in place, a young Bajan schoolboy pauses on his way home from classes near Belleplaine.

Images of Barbados

An island and its people

Text and photographs by
Roger LaBrucherie

Imágenes Press

The author wishes to thank the
following for their cooperation:

Jolly Roger Ltd.
Parasail Barbados Ltd.
Cooper Barbados, Ltd.
Barbados Foundry, Ltd.
Gordon Bain
Father Payne, St. John's Parish Church
Chris and Lawrie Gibbs
Randolph Field
Basil Forbes
Richard Goddard
Louis Stoskopf, Edgewater Hotel
Martha Hoch
and uncounted Bajans who were patient enough to pose for
me.

Foreword

But for poetic considerations this book would have been entitled Glimpses of Barbados, *for that is truly what these photographs represent: fleeting impressions of a land and its people.*

I am well aware that any book of this sort is a limited, and thus, necessarily, a biased portrayal. I make no apology for that; for if a photographer can be said to be in any way an artist, then surely it is primarily in his choice of subject matter.

Perhaps, then, "Images of Barbados" is best as a title, for it conveys the fact that these photographs are above all the personal viewpoint of the photographer.

If the reader perceives a bias toward depicting the people, as opposed to the scenery, of Barbados, I can only commend him for his perception, for therein lies my principal interest as a photographer. Further, I feel that this is the area most often slighted in books which are intended as a momento of a country.

In taking this approach, there is always the danger of looking for and recording only the picturesque, the colorful. . . . To surrender to this temptation inevitably means a work which trivializes a country, its people, and its culture. I hope that those who know Barbados well will judge that I have resisted the temptation.

El Centro, California, May, 1979

snapshots

Miss Ruth Ward stands with her son before her house in Bell Gully, St. Michael.

Barbadians have been called a nation of home-owners, and, indeed, nearly all live in single-family dwellings, apartment houses being a relative rarity.

Bajans may have the original "mobile homes" in their chattel houses, which rest on, but are not attached to, their foundations. (The latter often consist of no more than some precariously — but strategically! — placed rocks.) The practice has its origin in the fact that many Bajans own their homes, but not the land on which they rest — thus they can be readily moved to another site should the need arise.

Olivia

Cane fire!

A worker throws a bucket of water on an arsonist's blaze on a sugar estate near Oistins **(right)***. The effort proved futile, as young pranksters on the far side of the fire countered his efforts by throwing blazing cane into yet-unburnt areas. The arrival of a fire truck some minutes later saw the fire contained.*

Another, daytime, fire on the Kendall Estate **(this page)** *better shows the extent of the devastation. Recent years have seen sharp increases in total area burned, often at the hands of harvest workers whose work is speeded — and pay thereby increased — when fire strips the leaves, leaving the juice-bearing stalk unharmed. But the plantation owner, and the nation as a whole, loses, since syrup quality declines and production on burnt fields suffers in future years.*

Young boys on the beach at Oistins.

Weather-beaten perhaps, but the sign on this Bridgetown rumshop still reflects a pride in a long British heritage.

From the founding of the colony in 1627 until independence in 1966, British rule over the island was undisturbed. Aided by its geographical location and the difficulty of sailing square-rigged ships against the prevailing easterlies, a local militia and a British garrison succeeded in deterring attack during the era when France, Spain and England disputed Caribbean territory.

Today, many claim that this unbroken line of British rule and freedom from the effects of invasion and war account for the civility and mutual respect which mark the Barbadian character to such a degree.

Laden with a cartful of cane "meat" (the cane tops and leaves left in the field after the stalks are harvested), a donkey leads his master home at day's end. The meat will be used as fodder for the donkey itself and other livestock.

Once a major form of transport on the island, the quaint but ecologically-sound vehicles may have a brighter future than would have been imagined a few years ago.

Nimble-footed conductor rides the running-board of a "wood-pecker" bus (so nicknamed from the rattling of its wooden body), one of a vanishing breed.

The state-owned bus company charges one low fare for service anywhere on the island, a policy in keeping with the goal of minimizing a rural-urban migratory pattern which has already concentrated over half the country's population in the Bridgetown metropolitan area.

"Say cheese, darlin'," a friend calls out as Mrs. Eulalie Thorn tries to make a sale.

A fruit and vegetable vendor on the sidewalks of Speightstown, Mrs. Thorn stays in good spirits, although: "This is hard work, darlin', even if it looks easy. First you have to dig the vegetables and pick the fruit. Then sometimes you carry a 50-pound bundle a good long ways. And then you sit in one spot all day long – for a few dollars."

Pastor William Hunte with the congregation of the Mount Ebel Pentecostal Church of the United Holy Church of America, Coach Hill, St. John.

Small churches such as Pastor Hunte's are dotted throughout the villages and settlements of the island, reflecting the close attachment to religion shared by most Barbadians, especially the rural folk.

Ernetta Edghill runs "The Wee Wee Shop" in Foul Bay, St. Phillip: combination grocery, gossip exchange, pub, and sometime domino parlor.

It's hard to walk fifty yards in any settlement without encountering at least one such shop; they double as neighborhood social centers, where you're likely to run into a friend or relative, and always sure to find some lively conversation.

At one such shop in the parish of St. George my conversation with the owner led to an exchange of views on international relations, American movie stars, and Bajan racial harmony.

A group of young fellows finds the steps of a rumshop near Speightstown the perfect spot for "limin' out" (passing the time) on a warm afternoon.

Though a time-honored method of socializing, the custom is also symptomatic of the country's unemployment problem, especially among young men.

Bimshire

The East Point Lighthouse, on Ragged Point, at sunrise.

In photographing sunrises, there is no substitute for patience and good luck. This one came on the sixth-straight morning of pre-dawn awakenings and drives from Bridgetown.

A trace of dawn haze lingers over the East Coast, seen here from a point near Cherry Tree Hill. Early settlers avoided this coast, preferring the calmer waters of the Caribbean side, and for many years it remained a bit of a backwater. The isolation ended with the construction of a railroad in the 1880's (since abandoned) and the advent of modern all-weather highways.

The Morgan Lewis Mill greets the sun dawning over the Atlantic. The last windmill to retain its "points" and wheelhouse intact, the mill is now the property of the Barbados National Trust, an organization dedicated to the preservation of the Barbadian heritage.

Once over 500 such mills dotted the island's sugar estates, converting the steady trade winds into power for grinding the harvest. Steam-powered factories began replacing them in the 1840's, although one windmill remained in operation until 1946. Ironically, the country may once again turn to the wind to meet its power needs as the cost of alternative sources continues to rise.

Church bells sounding the hour, schoolgirls race across the courtyard of St. John's Parish Church on their way to morning classes.

In the tranquil churchyard, as within the church itself **(this page)**, the 17th-Century colonists who had come to call this island "Little England" were laid to rest. They had chosen the site for their church with poets' eyes: even today it is hard to wander among the headstones at the cliff's edge and gaze at the awe-filling view of the East Coast far below without thinking of how far they had come across a strange sea, to start a new land, and to end their lives. . . .

A college that sugar built: Codrington College provides training for the Anglican clergy in the West Indies.

The college owes its existence to a rather remarkable Barbadian, Christopher Codrington, whose radical ideas about slaves – that they were human beings who should be educated and instructed in Christianity – earned him the distrust and contempt of his fellow plantation owners in the 17th Century. At his death in 1710, his will provided for the establishment of a religious college on his estate overlooking Conset Bay, in St. John Parish.

Stormclouds threaten a Spring sky over Belleplaine and the surrounding Scotland District. Here the coral overlying most of the island gives way to the foundation strata of clays and sandstones; being impermeable to the heavy rains which fall from June through December, the region has eroded into sharp relief – hence the name, given by early colonists perhaps longing for their homeland.

A sea of cane, where once forests stood: by the 1670's – within 50 years of their arrival – the colonists had converted the island into a vast sugar factory. In so doing, they changed the human "face" of the island as well, for the plantations which quickly crowded out the small farmers soon discovered the value of African slaves for performing the arduous labor in the cane fields. Thus, just as the forests went, so did the white majority give way to an overwhelming black slave majority. Emancipation came in the 1840's, though true political power was not attained by the mass of the population until the mid-20th Century.

Built in the 1650's, Drax Hall (this page) shares with Nicholas Abbey the distinction of being the oldest plantation houses on the island. Clarence Shepherd, shown here with his wife, daughter and granddaughter, manages the estate – still one of the country's largest – for the descendants of James Drax, who is credited with introducing sugar cane to the island in the 1640's.

Bajans

Ashton Lane poses with his grandson Carlos at his home in Skeenes Hill (in the St. George Valley).

I came to know Ashton one day while out photographing scenes of cane harvesting; his home, like those of a great many rural Bajans, *is surrounded by cane fields, and his house rests on estate land.*

Just as his home is surrounded by cane, so has his life revolved around sugar cane, a relationship I encountered countless times in my meetings with country folk.

What makes a great athlete? To hear Sir Gary Sobers **(swinging bat)** *– perhaps the greatest cricket all-rounder of all time – tell it, above all: "dedication, hard work, discipline. . . ."*

I met him only briefly, on this day when he was counseling some young players at a coaching clinic, but I was struck, as I watched him work with the youngsters, by a quality which I could not quite describe, a quality not always found in the illustrious. . . .

"It's simple," one of his protégés told me as I gave him a lift home from the clinic, "He's a gentleman."

Yes, I think that's it.

A young man sits waiting for a bus near Dover, Christ Church.

In the Bajan style of dominoes, **form** *is as important as winning, which sometimes seems an afterthought; but the game wouldn't be complete without the whack!!! of pieces being slammed into place, echoing throughout the neighborhood.*

"I don't get around much anymore, but I'm pretty much content to stay home – what goes on downtown doesn't interest me like it did when I was younger." Mrs. Iris Humphrey's world in Top Rock, Christ Church, includes a house constantly full of neighbors and grandchildren, and a cheerful "All right, darlin' " to practically every passerby.

See and be seen is the rule on Broad Street on Saturday morning, as much of the populace turns out to do its shopping or simply do some browsing. This pretty high school student shows off the latest in coiffures.

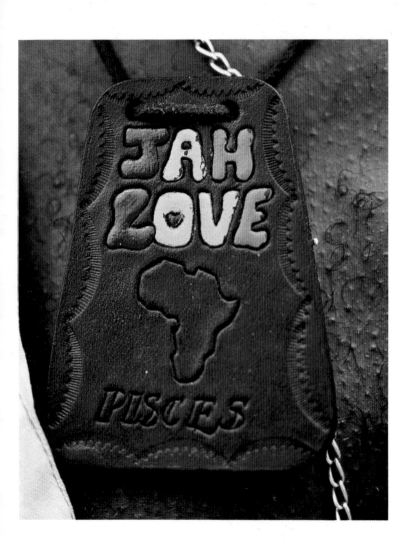

Focal point of controversy: a Ras Tafarian pauses en route to his peanut stand on Broad Street. Often identified by the "dreadlocks" worn in their hair, the "Rastas" (as they are commonly called in Barbados) take their name from the pre-coronation name of Ethiopia's Haile Selassie, who is worshipped as the Messiah and champion of the black race. The sect traces its origins to Jamaica but has spread throughout the Caribbean region, often stirring criticism for its doctrine of rejection of whites and European-based religion and culture. Still others point to Rastas as the source of a recent upsurge in theft.

Members of the sect and its defenders respond by pointing out the movement's doctrines of self-reliance, brotherly love toward all men, and a rejection of materialism — all inconsistent with criminal activity. Many youths having nothing to do with the sect, they claim, have adopted the "dreadlocks" as a mod style, and thus Rastas are often blamed for their activities.

A leather amulet worn by a Rasta, **(this page)** displays a medley of symbols, including the Ras Tafarian name for God, pride in African heritage, and the bearer's zodiacal sign.

island in the sun

Limbo!

A lithe performer delights a crowd at a popular nightspot outside Bridgetown **(left)**.

Origins of the dance are unclear; one theory maintains that it developed from gruesome necessity in the holds of slave ships, later to take hold as a folk dance in the West Indies. Whatever the source, the dance has become a standard Barbadian tourist attraction; the very best performers can pass below a flaming bar only eleven inches from the floor.

A fire-eater seems transfixed by a long tongue of flame **(below)**. These and other attractions have brought a boom in tourism and an increasing level of prosperity to Barbados just when income from sugar production, long the country's economic mainstay, has begun a decline. (In 1968 tourism for the first time surpassed sugar as a foreign exchange earner.) Thus tourism has become what Barbados had long sought, without great success: a second "crop" to reduce the hazards inherent in a one-crop economy.

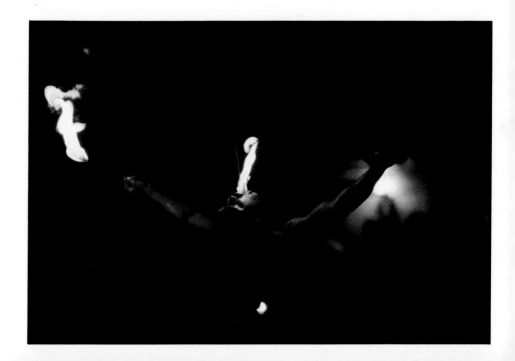

Horsepower of two different eras share the road to Holetown on the opening day of the annual Holetown Festival:

Having left their cares — and the snow — behind, winter visitors from Canada zip along the West Coast highway in a "Moke," the tourists' favored form of transportation.

Recalling a more genteel time, a gaily-decorated carriage and its escort make their way toward the Holetown Festival.

The two-day event features local artists, dancing, flower shows, and much more – all in commemoration of the island's first settlement by the English, in February, 1627.

Dangling eighty feet above the water, the author shoots a self-portrait and the Jolly Roger at anchor while parasailing off the coast at Holetown.

A modified parachute, an inboard-outboard boat, and a cooperative sea breeze permit standing starts and landings and a bird's-eye view of the popular resort area.

Well-oiled against sun-
burn and other con-
tingencies, a shipload of
tourists discoes under
the sails of the Jolly
Roger cruising off the
West Coast. Heeding
their captain's order that
"This is a fun cruise,
not a sightseeing
cruise," the mates-
for-a-day turn the ship
into a floating party.

Merrymakers dance to the tune of a "tuk" band of drums, flute and triangle in a parade during the Oistins Fish Festival, held each year in April. Gaily-adorned stalls offer games, drinks, souvenirs, and, of course, freshly-fried fish to a crowd drawn to the two-day celebration for the likes of boat races and fish-cleaning contests.

Though rustic in appearance, Oistins boasts a long and proud heritage: it was here, in 1652, that the "Charter of Barbados" – guaranteeing to Barbados a representative form of government – was signed by Oliver Cromwell's emissary.

For most of its 300-plus year history, the fishermen of Oistins have brought in their catch of flying fish, "dolphin" (dorado), and kingfish (wahoo) at sunset, just as they continue to do today **(opposite)**.

Perhaps entranced by the idyllic scene before him, a visitor sits lost in meditation on Accra Beach.

Whether for meditation, jogging, swimming, or just sun-soaking, the beaches and sun of Barbados are its sine qua non of tourism. Helped by direct charter flights from Canada, the USA and Europe, the country counted more than 300,000 tourists during 1978 — a number 20% greater than its own population.

As Barbados welcomes ever-increasing numbers of tourists, some Bajans may feel compelled, like this one, to fend off an identity crisis . . .

work

A young potter shapes a sample of his craft in his workshop in Chalky Mount, St. Andrew.

The region takes its nickname, "The Potteries," from the fact that its clay soils have supported generations of potters. Though the craftsmen have lost much of the local market to factory-produced goods, a growing tourist market has helped take up the slack.

A fiery dawn greets a cane cutter already at work on an estate in the St. George Valley. On a good day he may cut over seven tons, earning upwards of $35.00, a high wage compared to the other islands of the Caribbean. Even at this wage rate, however, plantation owners have difficulty in finding enough laborers for the backbreaking work; thus they turn to neighboring islands for temporary workers, and to mechanical harvesters, still being perfected. Since the 1640's the island's prosperity has depended on the size of the crop, and, even more importantly, on the price of sugar in the world market, characterized by erratic swings. The growth of tourism and efforts at industrialization have lately reduced the country's dependence on sugar.

Two feet long, weighing little more than a pound, a cane cutter's "collins" **(this page)** will be worn out by season's end in June; but the tool is well worth its five-dollar price: with it a top cutter may earn over $3000 during the six-month harvest.

Silhouetted against the fading western sky, the Foursquare Factory grinds on around the clock **(this page)**. *Ever-better land transport coupled with the greater efficiency of large mills promises to continue a trend toward fewer, larger mills: today fewer than ten factories grind a crop many times larger than that once ground by over 500 wind-driven mills.*

Technological advances in production meant ever-larger crops until recent years, when the loss of cane land to residential and industrial development has resulted in reduced production.

Employees on the swing shift clean a furnace at the Bulkeley Factory **(opposite)** *in St. George. Burning bagasse (the residue of cane stalks after the sugar-laden juice has been squeezed out) enables the mills to completely supply their own power needs.*

A technician at the Bulkeley Factory checks crystal formation in a batch of syrup from the vacuum pan. In modern mills such as this one, sugar-to-cane ratios as high as 1:8.5 (by weight) are achieved, depending on the quality of the cane.

Beset by low prices in the world market caused by over-production, industry researchers explore alternative uses for cane: already in Brazil cane is being processed into alcohol to fuel cars. In Barbados a test plant experiments with the conversion of bagasse into wallboard.

A crew of workers weeds a cane field on an estate near Bushy Park, St. Phillip. In Barbados the great bulk of agricultural work is carried out by women, although men do most of the cane cutting and operate equipment.

The reasons, at least in part: a greater number of men than women have emigrated, leaving women in the majority in all adult age groups; and the great number of women who are the sole support of their children.

Wharfside at the Careenage, an inter-island freighter off-loads a shipment of flour. Larger ships use the modern Deep Water Harbour, but small vessels and the Capital's fishing fleet continue to moor in the heart of the city, to the delight of tourists and photographers.

The domination of arable land by sugar cultivation, coupled with a high population density, means the country must import a large part of its food. Such imports, along with petroleum and luxury goods, have created serious trade deficits in recent years. The government counts on tourism and industrial development, plus agricultural diversification, to improve the trade situation.

A merchant seaman gazes from a window of the MV Ana Sexta, *in for repairs at the Careenage. An island geography, a British heritage, and shortage of employment on land* have led many Barbadians to the seafaring life. The wages saved from years at sea have often provided the capital for acquiring land, a Barbadian passion.

Workers at the Barbados Foundry cast a three-ton roller (grinder) for a sugar factory. In addition to rollers, the foundry fabricates a number of other parts for the factory machinery, thus making the island largely self-sufficient in its sugar production.

Hockey gloves in the tropics?! An employee of Cooper Barbados Ltd., subsidiary of a Canadian sporting goods manufacturer, puts the finishing touches on a glove destined for export. The company is one of dozens lured to the island under a program managed by the Industrial Development Corporation, aimed at economic diversification and job development.

"Sure, the tax incentives and wage scales were attractive to us," a spokesman for one company told me, "but there were other factors as well – after all, there are other countries with lower wages. The stability of the country, the quality of the labor force, and absence of corruption in government . . . all these influenced our coming here. And we're glad we did – we're planning an expansion."

A roughneck wrestles with a mile-long drill pipe to change a worn bit on a flood-lit oil rig near Searles, Christ Church.

Already self-sufficient in natural gas, the country has hopes of further reducing its oil import costs by continued development of this and other small fields.

little ones

"Take my picture!" shouted these children I passed in Six Cross Roads. And so I did.

Full of mischief and fun, the omnipresent children of Barbados are both a delight and a symbol of one of Barbados' continuing challenges: the press of an ever-growing population on an already-crowded island. The situation would be even more acute were it not for large emigrations which occurred throughout this century, beginning with the large outflow of workers who helped build the

Panama Canal. Today tens of thousands of Bajans live in both North America and England, but the increasingly restrictive immigration policies of many nations today means that the work of the Family Planning Association becomes ever more important. Already its efforts have helped bring about a 30% reduction in the birth rate in the past 15 years.

Recess time for a class of kindergarten-age urchins at a school in Bridgetown.

Choirboys await the signal for the commencement of morning services at St. Michael's Cathedral, seat of the Anglican Church in Barbados. Until 1970 the Church was the established religion in the country; since that time all religions are on an equal footing, and complete freedom of religion has historically prevailed..

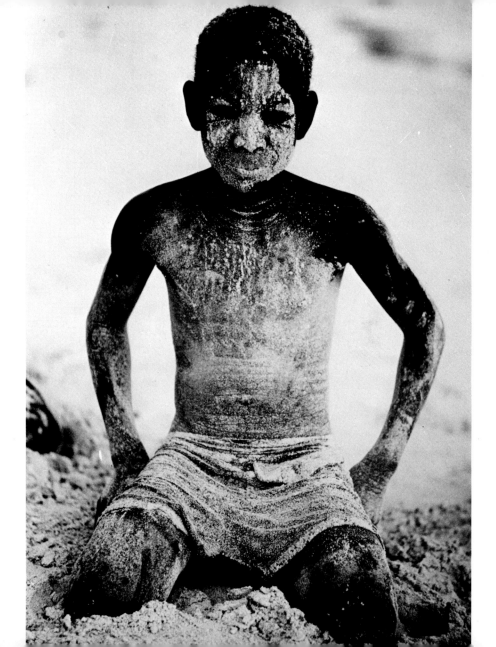

A sand-covered boy mugs the camera on the beach near Speightstown.

The task of carrying water home from the village standpipe often falls to the young boys in a family. . . .

Beyond such household chores, only a tiny minority (less than 1%) of Barbadian children are in the labor force. A relatively high standard of living, aided by remittances from relatives living abroad, and universal free education enable essentially all children to attend school.

A classroom of third-graders at the Boscobelle Girls' School in St. Peter.

Barbados claims a literacy rate of 97%, one of the world's highest. Education is free to all qualified students through the college level.

Many schools are purposely situated outside the Bridgetown metropolitan area, thus reducing the strain on the sometimes-overwhelmed public transport system.

Young girl in a doorway on Nelson Street, Bridgetown.

Though Barbados has its rich and its poor, the gap between the two is far smaller than that found in most "developing" nations. Indeed, a person familiar with underdeveloped countries is struck by the absence of slums, and the fact that nearly all houses have electricity and a large percentage have running water. No wonder many people argue that Barbados, with a per capita annual income of over US$1500, no longer belongs in the category of "developing country" at all.

Elena

For children everywhere, the Sunday sermon may become a little wearisome . . . these young members of the congregation pass the moment watching the antics of a photographer across the road.

details

Relic of an ancient past, symbols of a continuing heritage:

The zemi (this page) *is a rare surviving reminder that Barbados was once home to a civilization long vanished from the island*

when the English arrived. The Arawaks, a peaceful people who lived by fishing and agriculture, communicated with their deities through these figurines carved from coral. Their presence on the island gave way about 1200 A.D. to the more warlike Carib Indians, who inhabited the island through the 16th Century. It is very likely that the Carib population on the island was decimated by Spanish raiding parties who enslaved them to work the mines and plantations of Hispaniola, for there is no record of the English — who arrived in 1627 — having encountered an Indian population.

Symbols of old ties, still strong: Becky Gibbs, the daughter of a Barbadian-Canadian marriage, poses next to a mailbox (opposite) *dating from the days when Barbados was still a British colony. Since 1966 an independent country within the British Commonwealth of Nations, Barbados continues to recognize* Elizabeth Regina II *as its head of state.*

"Independence was in some ways like gaining adulthood," one Bajan explained it to me, when I wondered aloud why Barbados had remained within the Commonwealth, "You don't renounce your family name or ties just because you're out on your own."

From all appearances, the vast majority of Bajans seem content with the arrangement which continues to link them with Britain, Canada, and the other Commonwealth countries.

(Zemi courtesy of the Roach Collection.)

The piercing nighttime calls of Eleutherodactylus martinicensis, *the thumbnail-sized "whistling" frog, often startles and bewilders first-time visitors to the island — especially if they find one sharing the shower uninvited!*

Caesalpinia pulcher-
rima, *"Pride of Bar-
bados,"* the national
flower.

Barbados is a **coral island**, the guidebooks remind us, and, indeed, the organisms whose skeletons formed the surface of most of the island continue to grow in the waters around Barbados. Some, like this black coral brought from depths as great as 200 feet, is fashioned into jewelry.

Recipe for a memorable Bajan meal: take flying fish, rice and peas, a christophine salad, and set a table with a view overlooking the East Coast . . .

Bridgetown

A doorway shadows a sidewalk fruit vendor, one of hundreds lending color to the Capital's streets.

"Yes, the government built some covered markets for us," one lady confided to me, "but this is where the people are, and if you don't go where the people are, you don't sell nothing. Besides, I like to see what's going on."

A "banana boat" pulls into the Careenage, and the word quickly spreads to a small army of vendors, who converge for spirited bargaining for bananas, plantains, and mangoes.

In the background stand the Public Buildings (built in the 1870's after a fire that devastated central Bridgetown), which house government departments, including the Post Office and Parliament. Today's Parliament is a continuation of the House of Assembly, which first met in 1639, thus laying claim to being one of the oldest representative bodies in the New World.

A pair of fishermen share a quiet conversation as the sun settles over the Careenage, as Bridgetown's historic harbour is named.

The center point of Bridgetown's commercial life, the Careenage has been central to her *history as well. Though Holetown was first settled, the superiority of Bridgetown's natural harbour quickly caused it to surpass its northern rival in importance, and it has remained the undisputed political, economic, and social center of the island.*

Impetuous, quick to laugh, full of life – and above all, the quintessential British hero – no wonder he captured the hearts of Barbadians, and holds them to this day. Within days of learning of his death and victory over the Spanish and French at Cape Trafalgar, a collection for a memorial was begun; and so, for the last century and a half Horatio, Lord Nelson has stood serenely in Trafalgar Square and surveyed the passing scene.

Parishoners leave Sunday services at St. Michael's Cathedral (Anglican), which dates from 1789. The original church on this site was destroyed in 1780 during one of the violent hurricanes which has periodically wreaked great damage on the island.

The Established Church of the island for most of its history, the Anglican faith continues to attract the greatest number of adherents, although today over a score of different faiths coexist in Barbados.

Early morning shadows steal across Baxter's Road as Bridgetown stirs to life. Full of commerce by day, at night the street gives way to stalls where fried fish can be bought through the early hours of the morning.

Small buildings and narrow streets belie the fact that the city houses a population of more than 80,000.

Shops on Suttle Street recall the face that central Bridgetown wore before giving way to modern steel and concrete. Most of the old wooden buildings have fallen to fires which have periodically swept the area.

Beckwith Street.

more Bajans

All eyes rivet the ball at a tense moment in a West Indies-Australia match at Kensington Oval.

More national passion than pastime, cricket nearly monopolizes the country's attention dur- *ing an important match; transistor radios pressed to hundreds of ears on street corners, on buses, in shops, are a sure sign that a West Indies team is contesting a match somewhere in the world.*

Perhaps contemplating a long road traveled from his days of playing street cricket, a promising young batsman waits his turn before the wicket during trials to select the Barbadian national team for a West Indies tournament.

Long a "gentleman's sport," only in the recent past have financial support and the prospect of touring with professional teams made cricket a viable option for Barbadians of all economic levels.

Tools at his shoulder, a workman heads for his job on a road crew in the Scotland District.

A serious unemployment problem – rates have reached as high as 15% in recent years – has prompted the government to adopt an extensive program of public works and maintenance. Despite these efforts, the situation is likely to remain grave: nearly 40% of the population is under 15 years of age, thus promising a rapidly-growing labor force in search of employment.

Sometimes it seems that every house in Barbados has someone at a window, watching the passing scene. I captured this scene in Sturges, St. Thomas Parish.

The delight of tourists, a Harbour Policeman's 19th-century uniform belies the fact that he is a working constable of the Royal Barbados Police Force. Unarmed, in the British tradition, the weight of the authority he represents is all the force he needs in this essentially peaceful society where the crime rate has remained astonishingly low.

endings

Pico Teneriffe, dawn.

Late afternoon shadow and the pounding Atlantic provide the setting for a tranquil walk along the East Coast.

St. John's Parish Church.

Strollers watch the finale to a February day on Dover Beach.

From a photographic standpoint, the picture on the facing page is not a spectacular one, and yet, I knew from the moment I took it that it would close this book, for the Barbadians in it are special to me, and still they are typical of scores of Bajans I met.

I came to know Ronald and Milda Tull one morning when I was on the East Coast scouting sunrise scenics. There are few cafes in the rural areas of Barbados, and virtually none open at 6 a.m., so I developed the habit on these early-morning excursions of stopping at private homes to ask to buy a cup of coffee or tea. The one I chose on that morning was one of the more rustic in Barbados; the lady of the house was doing her breakfast dishes on the back step. She asked me to have a seat and said that her husband would fix a cup of tea for me. I sat down on a large boulder in the back yard; while I waited I wondered how much I should offer to pay for the tea.

Several minutes passed and Ronald came out of the house with a tray bearing tea, sausage, and biscuits.

Perhaps it was the hour, or the fact that this was obviously not a wealthy household, or my own parsimonious thoughts of minutes before, but this simple act of generosity overwhelmed me (for they refused to accept anything in payment). When I told them so, Ronald replied simply: "I just do like my mother always did with strangers."

We talked a long while: Ronald was a mechanic by trade; their baby, Anderson, was then just three months old, and they proudly showed him off. I explained what I was doing in Barbados, and I asked them if they would be willing to appear in this book. I feared they would refuse – I had long since discovered that many Bajans strongly dislike being photographed – and indeed, Milda declined. I asked if I might return another day to show them an earlier book I had done, with the hope that they might change their minds.

Several days later I went back to show them the book. They both looked through it, silently; then Ronald handed it back, saying, "I'm sorry, but I think Milda's still unwilling."

My face undoubtedly showed my disappointment as I thanked them for considering it, bid them farewell, and turned to go – when I heard Milda say, "I don't see the harm in it." I smiled a thank you and hurried to get my cameras. This is the picture that resulted.

I hope Milda will not regret having changed her mind.

Notes

The term "Bajan" is a common expression in use in Barbados to mean "Barbadian"; I have used it frequently in the text.

The term "Bimshire" to mean Barbados has a long and uncertain history; the word "Bim" is, similarly, an old expression meaning Barbadian, of which the origin is uncertain. However, once the latter term developed, it is easy to see how the affectionate term "Bimshire" would evolve to designate an island so closely tied to England.

In all cases where the dollar sign ($) alone is used, it is the Barbadian dollar which is referred to (1979 value: about two Barbadian dollars equal one U.S. dollar).

Photographic Notes

There are many good cameras and films. I worked with Agfachrome and Nikon equipment (Nikon F2S, Nikkormat FTN and EL bodies, and with various Nikkor lenses between 18mm and 500mm in focal length).

I use Nikon equipment for one principal reason: I believe they are unmatched for ruggedness and reliability. When you are working rapidly with more than one body and several lenses, equipment can get banged around quite a bit. One time in Barbados I was making a hurried lens change at a cricket match when one lens flew out of my hand and dropped perhaps a foot onto a concrete floor.

There was a slight dent in the lens hood; otherwise the lens was unharmed. I have other such stories, all of which convince me that the lengendary ruggedness is not just legend.

I am sorry to disappoint those who like to see exposure information for each photograph; I've found that noting down exposures in this type of photography is simply impractical. Besides, in the great majority of cases the direct meter reading was used; in tricky light a lot of bracketed exposures is the technique most likely to ensure success.

Photo by Arthur Warman

Writer-photographer and friend: Roger LaBrucherie is a lawyer by training and a native of El Centro, California. This is his second book.

His "friend," a baby black-bellied or "hair" sheep (often mistaken by visitors for goats) is a common sight grazing along the roadsides of Barbados. An African import, the breed is well-suited to the tropics and helps make efficient use of soils too shallow or too dry to support anything but grass.

Imágenes Press
P.O. Box 653
El Centro, California 92244 USA
Tel: (619) 352-2188

Printed in China

ISBN 0-939302-01-2